DAMAGED FINANCES: Why Our Monetary System is Letting Us Down and How We Can Make It Persuasive

By

SHAWN J. BURLESON

DISCLAIMER

TABLE OF CONTENT

Contents

INTRODUCTION

Money is an everyday element of our lives. We utilize money to purchase food, pay rent, save for the future, and realize our aspirations. It's a means of exchange that powers the engine of our global economy, making it possible for us to trade goods and services, form enterprises, and pursue pleasure. Yet, how often do we pause and think about the monetary system that underlies it all?

In this book, "DAMAGED FINANCES: Why Our Monetary System is Letting Us Down and How We Can Make It Persuasive," we'll begin on a trip to investigate the intricate network of our monetary system, understand its complexity, and expose its influence on our everyday lives.

The Significance of the Monetary System:

The monetary system isn't simply a matter for economists and policymakers; it's something that touches us all, from the moment we receive our first allowance as youngsters until our retirement years. Think about it: every time you earn a salary, swipe your credit card, or stow away money in your savings account, you're dealing with the monetary system.

The money you have in your wallet or see digitally on your bank statement is a representation of the health of our monetary system. It represents the worth of your effort, your capacity to provide for your family, and your hopes for the future. Therefore, understanding how this system operates and the issues it faces is vital for making educated financial decisions and maintaining your economic well-being.

<u>**The Purpose and Scope of the Book:**</u> The objective of this work is twofold. Firstly, it tries to shed light on the underlying workings of our monetary system in a way that's accessible to everyone, regardless of your background or prior understanding of economics.

You don't need to be an expert to grasp the topics we'll discuss; we'll break them down into plain, easy-to-understand language. Secondly, this book aims to address the key concerns affecting our monetary system today.

From the prospect of inflation and growing economic disparity to the looming threat of debt problems, we'll dig into the difficulties that affect people, families, and entire nations. But we won't stop at merely pointing out the faults; we'll also provide actual answers and roads to a more convincing monetary system.

<u>Preview of Key Themes and Arguments:</u> Throughout the pages that follow, we'll study the historical history of money, the duties of central banks, and the impact of inflation on our purchasing power. We'll investigate alternative monetary systems like cryptocurrency and discuss their

benefits and downsides. We'll also hear the experiences of individuals whose lives have been influenced by financial issues under the present system. As we go, we'll suggest modifications to our monetary system and underscore the necessity of financial education in equipping individuals to navigate the financial world efficiently.

We'll examine examples of countries that have successfully altered their monetary systems and the lessons we may learn from them. By the end of this trip, we hope you'll not only have a broader grasp of our monetary system but also feel inspired and equipped to contribute to discussions about its future. Our mission is to equip you to fight for a more equal, stable, and compelling monetary system that benefits us all. So, let's begin on this informative voyage together and study the world of finances, money, and the monetary system. The adventure begins here.

CHAPTER 1

THE FOUNDATIONS OF MONEY

Money is the lifeblood of our modern civilization. It's what we use to buy products, pay for services, and save for the future. But how did we get here? How did we move from old barter systems to today's complicated financial world? In this chapter, we'll embark on a trip through time to unearth the intriguing history of money, grasp its basic functions in our lives, and gain a look into the complicated world of monetary systems.

Historical Evolution of Money

From Barter to Bills: The Remarkable Journey Imagine a world without money, when people had to sell products directly. You could have a sack of wheat and need a new pair of shoes. In a barter system, you'd have to locate a shoemaker who not only required your wheat but also had shoes that fit you. It's a difficult procedure, to say the least.

<u>trade Systems:</u> In the earliest human cultures, trade was the principal mode of commerce. People transferred products and

services directly, relying on a mutual need for what the other person had to give. However, barter has its limitations. It needed a double coincidence of wants, meaning both parties had to want what the other possessed at the same moment.

The Emergence of Commodity Money:

To address the limits of barter, cultures began to employ commodity money items with inherent worth that were generally recognized as vehicles of trade.

Examples included animals, food, and even seashells. These goods had worth in themselves, making commerce simpler.

The Birth of Coins: Around 600 BCE, the

first metal coins appeared in the kingdom of

Lydia (modern-day Turkey). These coins, fashioned from electrum (a naturally occurring alloy of gold and silver), constituted a tremendous leap in the history of money. They had standardized weights and values, making trading more efficient.

Paper Money and Banking: As civilizations flourished and trade expanded, carrying huge bags of metal currency became cumbersome. In response, Chinese merchants in the 7th century CE began employing paper money as a symbol of stored value. Meanwhile, medieval European banks started producing promissory notes, effectively IOUs, that could be traded as if they were money.

Key Milestones and Innovations:

Throughout history, numerous civilizations contributed to the evolution of money. The Roman Empire established the notion of a uniform currency, the denarius. In the Middle Ages, Italian financial firms pioneered the use of bills of trade. The Renaissance witnessed the first checks and the foundation of modern banking institutions.

The Rise of Fiat Money:

By the 17th century, many governments had moved away from commodity money and adopted fiat money currency, not backed by a real product but acknowledged as legal tender by government edict. This move created the basis for today's monetary systems.

The Role of Money in Modern Economies

Money as the Engine of Trade In the contemporary world, money performs three key tasks that make our complicated economies run smoothly: it's a medium of trade, a unit of account, and a store of value.

Medium of Exchange: Money is the bridge that permits us to exchange. Instead of trying to locate someone who wants exactly what we have to give, we may swap money for products and services, streamlining transactions.

Unit of Account: Money offers a standard measure for valuing commodities and services. It allows us to compare the price of a loaf of bread to a gallon of milk, a smartphone, or a car. This single unit makes economic decisions and financial planning more approachable.

Store of Value: Money permits us to save and store riches for the future. We can lay away money now, sure that it will preserve its worth over time. This function of money is crucial for long-term financial planning, retirement savings, and investment.

Introduction to Monetary Systems

The Architects of Economic Stability Now that we've covered the historical journey of money and its vital functions in our lives, let's turn our attention to the notion of monetary systems and why they matter.

<u>Monetary Systems Defined:</u> A monetary system is like the conductor of an orchestra, regulating the flow of money in an economy. It covers the laws, organizations, and systems that regulate the creation, circulation, and regulation of money. Essentially, it's the foundation that guarantees money functions successfully.

<u>Significance of Monetary Systems:</u> Monetary systems are not simply about printing banknotes and minting coins; they are the backbone of economic stability. They impact the money supply (the quantity of money circulating in an economy), interest rates, and general financial soundness. A well-functioning monetary system may foster economic growth, whereas a badly managed one can lead to crises.

Monetary Policy: At the center of each monetary system is monetary policy. This is the toolkit that central banks and governments employ to control the economy. Monetary policy encompasses choices on interest rates, money supply, and other factors that impact the availability and value of money.

How Monetary Policy Works: Imagine a seesaw. On one side, you have inflation the rising costs of goods and services. On the other side, you have unemployment, which is the number of individuals without work. Monetary policy seeks to balance these two tendencies.

When inflation threatens to become too high, central banks may raise interest rates to dampen spending. Conversely, when unemployment is a problem, central banks could cut interest rates to stimulate borrowing and spending.

Controlling the Money Supply: One of the key duties of monetary policy is regulating the money supply. Central banks employ several methods to achieve this, such as open market operations (buying or selling government bonds), adjusting the reserve requirements for banks, and setting interest rates.

By altering these levers, they can affect how much money is circulating in the economy. Impact on Interest Rates: Interest rates are the cost of borrowing money. When central banks raise interest rates, it becomes more costly to borrow, which might slow down consumption and investment. Conversely, decreasing interest rates increase borrowing and investment, promoting economic growth.

<u>**Balancing Act:**</u> Managing a monetary system is a difficult balancing act. Central banks must be alert, keeping an eye on inflation, unemployment, and other economic indicators. Their purpose is to keep the economy stable, ensuring that money keeps its value and individuals have the chance to find work. In the chapters that follow, we'll dig further into the complicated realm of monetary systems. We'll explore the

issues they face, their influence on our lives, and the opportunity for reform. By understanding the fundamentals of money and monetary systems, you'll be better able to navigate the complicated financial environment and make educated decisions that determine your financial destiny.

CHAPTER 2

THE CURRENT MONETARY SYSTEM

In the last chapter, we covered the historical path of money, from its humble beginnings in barter systems to the complex financial world we occupy today. Now, it's time to plunge into the core of our modern financial system: the present monetary system. In this chapter, we'll take a deeper look at how our monetary system runs, the vital role of central banks, and the main individuals that keep the wheels of finance rolling.

Overview of the Existing Monetary System Fiat Currency and Central Banking:

The Backbone of Our Financial World The present monetary system, which sustains the global economy, is constructed on two basic pillars: fiat money and central banks.

Fiat Currency Defined:

In the current world, most money exists as fiat currency. Unlike commodity money (such as gold or silver coins), fiat currency has no intrinsic value. It is valued because a government proclaims it to be legal tender, meaning it must be recognized as a means of trade inside that country.

The Role of Central Banks: The central bank is the protector of our monetary system. They are responsible for issuing and managing the money supply, setting interest rates, and preserving financial stability.

Money Supply: Central banks have the authority to create and destroy money. They achieve this through different means, including establishing reserve requirements for commercial banks, purchasing and selling government assets, and influencing interest rates.

<u>Interest Rates:</u> Central banks play a crucial role in managing interest rates. By altering the benchmark interest rate (such as the federal funds rate in the United States), they impact the cost of borrowing money, which, in turn, influences expenditure and investment.

<u>Financial Stability:</u> Central banks are also responsible for preserving financial stability. They monitor the health of commercial banks, act during crises, and establish rules to avert systemic hazards.

<u>Central Banks and Their Roles:</u> The Maestros of Monetary Policy Central banks are sometimes referred to as the "lenders of last resort" and the "conductors of the orchestra" in the world of finance.

Let's go deeper into their duties and functions.

Monetary Policy: The fundamental job of central banks is to administer monetary policy. This entails making decisions that affect the money supply, interest rates, and, eventually, the general health of the economy.

Interest Rates: Central banks govern short-term interest rates by establishing the benchmark rate. They do this to achieve numerous economic goals, such as price stability (keeping inflation in line) and full employment.

Open Market Operations: One of the methods central banks employ to execute monetary policy is open market operations. This entails purchasing and selling government assets on the open market to impact the money supply.

Reserve Requirements: Central banks can also establish reserve requirements for commercial banks. This regulates the proportion of deposits that banks must retain in reserve. By altering these restrictions, central banks can impact the amount of money banks can lend.

Bank supervision: Central banks monitor the activities of commercial banks within their authority. They guarantee that banks run soundly, don't take unnecessary risks, and have adequate capital to withstand financial shocks.

<u>Financial Stability:</u> Central banks are the first line of defense against financial crises. They offer emergency funding to banks suffering liquidity concerns and take precautions to avert financial panics. Currency Rates: In certain nations, central banks are responsible for maintaining currency rates. They may interfere in foreign exchange markets to stabilize their country's currency.

<u>Key Players in the Monetary System:</u>

An Orchestra of Finance The monetary system is not a solitary performance; it's a symphony with numerous musicians. Let's meet the important stakeholders who shape our financial environment.

Commercial Banks: Commercial banks are the mediators between central banks and the general population. They collect deposits from people and corporations and provide loans and financial services. Banks play a crucial role in the money creation process through fractional reserve banking.

Financial Markets: Financial markets are where the buying and selling of financial assets occur. This encompasses stock markets, bond markets, commodity markets, and currency markets. These markets determine asset values, interest rates, and exchange rates.

International Monetary Fund (IMF): The IMF is an international institution that offers financial aid, policy advice, and technical help to member nations confronting balance of payments concerns. It fosters international monetary cooperation and exchange rate stability.

World Bank: The World Bank is another international financial agency that gives loans and grants to the world's poorest countries. Its purpose is to eradicate poverty and promote sustainable economic growth.

Treasury Departments: Government Treasury Departments are responsible for issuing government bonds and managing government debt. They work closely with central banks to guarantee the government's borrowing requirements are satisfied.

Financial Regulators: In addition to central banks, financial regulators play a significant role in monitoring financial institutions and markets. They implement rules and regulations to ensure market integrity and safeguard customers.

Financial Institutions: Besides commercial banks, other financial institutions, including investment banks, insurance firms, and credit unions, are part of the financial ecosystem. They provide a wide range of financial services and products.

Consumers and businesses: At the center of the monetary system are individuals and corporations. Their decisions regarding spending, saving, investing, and borrowing together impact the economy.

<u>The worldwide interconnection:</u> The current monetary system is strongly integrated on a worldwide basis. Exchange rates, trade, and financial flows transcend boundaries, making the coordination of monetary policy across countries vital for stability. As we continue our investigation of the existing monetary system, we'll look into its strengths and faults, the issues it confronts, and the various avenues for reform. Understanding this dense network of financial actors and organizations is vital for making educated decisions in an increasingly complex financial environment. So, let's journey further into this fascinating domain of finance, where the acts of central banks, the judgments of financial markets, and the choices of individuals all join together to build our economic reality.

CHAPTER 3

THE PROBLEMS WITH OUR MONETARY SYSTEM

As we explore further into the complicated realm of our monetary system, it's time to put a focus on some of the critical difficulties it confronts. While the monetary system serves a critical role in fueling economic growth and stability, it is not without its problems. In this chapter, we'll analyze four significant difficulties that our monetary system grapples with: inflation, income inequality, debt crises, and a lack of openness. We'll examine how these challenges affect individuals and economies and why they deserve our attention.

Inflation and its Impact

Rising Prices and the Erosion of Purchasing Power Inflation is a phrase we commonly hear in economic talks, but what does it truly imply, and why should we care?

Understanding Inflation: At its heart, inflation refers to the general increase in prices over time. When prices rise, each unit of currency buys fewer products and services. This means that the money in your wallet now may not have the same purchasing power in the future.

<u>Causes of inflation:</u> Inflation may be induced by several reasons, including increased demand for products and services, rising production costs (such as labor and raw materials), and changes in government policy, such as excessive money printing.

<u>ramifications of inflation:</u> The ramifications of inflation are far-reaching. It can decrease the real value of savings, making it difficult for individuals to prepare for their future. It can also affect economic decision-making as individuals hurry to spend money rather than save it.

<u>Real-World Impact:</u> Let's explore a real-world example. Suppose you're intending to buy a car for $20,000, and you've saved for a year. However, due to inflation, the price of the automobile increases by 5% throughout the year. Suddenly, your $20,000 is only worth $19,000 in terms of purchasing power, making it more difficult to finance the automobile you had your sights on.

Income Inequality: The Monetary System's Role in Wealth Disparities Income inequality is a hot-button subject that is directly tied to our monetary system. Let's analyze how monetary policies may either worsen or relieve income gaps.

The Monetary System's Influence: The monetary system has a role in income inequality through its influence on asset values, interest rates, and access to financial opportunities.

Asset values: When central banks implement policies like low interest rates to boost economic growth, it frequently leads to greater asset values, such as real estate and equities. Others that hold these assets gain from the price appreciation, while others without them lose out.

Interest Rates: Low interest rates can make it cheaper for firms to borrow money for expansion or investment, thus contributing to job creation. However, they can also lead to decreased returns on savings, harming individuals who rely on interest income.

Access to Financial Possibilities: The availability of credit and financial possibilities might vary greatly. People with solid credit histories and assets can receive loans at favorable rates, while those without collateral or credit incur higher borrowing expenses.

Debt crises and financial instability

The Domino Effect of Unsustainable Debt Debt crises and financial instability are recurrent nightmares that have tormented countries throughout the world. In this part, we'll analyze the relationship between our monetary system and these perilous situations.

<u>**The Role of Debt:**</u> Debt is a double-edged sword. When utilized wisely, money can promote economic growth by providing individuals and businesses with the capital they need to invest and expand. However,

excessive debt can lead to financial instability.

How Debt Can Spiral: Imagine a world where people and organizations amass debt at a fast pace. They become heavily leveraged, meaning they owe more than they can safely repay. If an economic shock happens, such as a recession, these borrowers may struggle to satisfy their commitments, leading to defaults.

The 2008 Financial Crisis: The 2008 financial crisis provides a clear example of how debt issues may generate financial instability. The increasing usage of sophisticated financial instruments related to mortgages led to a cascading series of defaults, finally ending in a worldwide financial crisis.

Impact on Society: Debt crises can have serious implications for society. They can lead to job losses, house foreclosures, and the erosion of retirement assets. Governments typically step in with bailouts to stabilize the financial system, but this may come at a significant cost to taxpayers.

Lack of transparency

The Veil of Secrecy in Monetary Policy Transparency is a vital cornerstone of confidence in our monetary system. When central banks and financial institutions work behind closed doors, it can damage public trust and raise concerns about their decision-making.

The Importance of Transparency:

Transparency in monetary policy implies that central banks communicate their aims, tactics, and decisions openly to the public. This transparency helps the public comprehend the logic behind policy actions.

Concerns About openness: Critics

contend that central banks and financial organizations often lack openness in their activities. For example, they may not reveal essential information about their decision-making processes, or they may not give adequate insight into the reasons behind policy measures.

<u>The Role of Trust:</u> Trust is crucial in the monetary system. When consumers and companies trust that central banks are functioning in the best interests of the economy, they are more likely to have confidence in the system and make prudent financial decisions.

<u>The case for openness:</u> Proponents of openness claim that it helps central banks be more responsible to the public and prevents excessive influence from financial interests. It also provides for better predictability in financial markets, lowering uncertainty.

In this chapter, we've revealed some of the underlying flaws that afflict our monetary system. Inflation erodes our purchasing power, income inequality generates inequities, debt crises can lead to financial instability, and a lack of transparency can erode public trust. As we move forward, we'll investigate various ways to solve these concerns and establish a more robust and egalitarian monetary system. Understanding these difficulties is the first step toward discovering effective treatments that benefit us all.

CHAPTER 4

HISTORICAL PERSPECTIVES ON MONETARY SYSTEM

To really appreciate the issues and potential solutions in our current monetary system, it's necessary to investigate past instances. Throughout the millennia, different monetary systems have arisen, each with its own distinct qualities and implications. In this chapter, we'll start on a trip through time, covering case studies such as the gold standard, bimetallism, and alternative currency systems. By understanding the strengths and shortcomings of these historical trials, we may draw useful insights to aid us in determining the future of our monetary system.

Explore historical examples.

Unveiling the Monetary Systems of the Past Historical monetary systems offer us significant insights into the evolution of money and finance.

Let's go into the specifics of a few major examples:

The Gold Standard

The Lustrous Standard of Monetary Stability The gold standard was one of the most significant monetary regimes in history. It functioned on the concept that the value of a nation's currency was directly related to a certain quantity of gold.

Characteristics of the Gold Standard:

Under the gold standard, each unit of

currency, such as the dollar or pound, was backed by an equal quantity of gold kept in the country's reserves. This pegging of currency to gold ensured stability, as the money supply was restricted by the available gold.

<u>Reasons for Adoption:</u> The gold standard brought various advantages, including price stability and faith in the currency. It also promoted international trade since currencies could be freely swapped based on their gold values.

<u>The Downfall of the Gold Standard:</u> Despite its benefits, the gold standard had limitations. During economic crises, governments typically experience deflationary pressures since they can't grow

the money supply to combat recessions. Additionally, the fixed supply of gold hindered economic expansion.

Bimetallism

The Dual Metal Monetary System Bimetallism was another ancient monetary system that depended on two precious metals, often gold and silver, to serve as the basis for money.

Characteristics of Bimetallism: In a bimetallic system, both gold and silver coins were in circulation, with fixed exchange values between the two metals. This allowed for greater flexibility in the money supply.

<u>Reasons for Adoption:</u> Bimetallism tried to remedy some of the problems of the gold standard. It gave more flexibility in responding to variations in the supply of gold and silver and accommodated economic expansion.

<u>**issues of bimetallism:**</u> Bimetallism had issues relating to maintaining stable exchange rates between gold and silver, as market forces often drove the prices of the two metals in different directions.

<u>Alternative currency systems</u>

Innovative Approaches to Money Throughout history, several alternative currency systems have evolved, frequently in reaction to economic crises or specific conditions. **Characteristics of Alternative Currency Systems:** These systems can take numerous forms, such as local complementary currencies, time-based currencies, or digital cryptocurrencies. They strive to facilitate trade and develop communal exchange.

Reasons for Adoption: Alternative currency systems sometimes develop in times of economic turmoil or as a tool to boost local economies and social harmony. For example, local complementary currencies stimulate spending within a given community.

Success Stories: Some alternative currency systems have achieved success in accomplishing their intended purposes, such as the Swiss WIR or the digital currency Bitcoin. These systems frequently thrive on trust and community support.

Lessons Learned from Past Monetary Experiments

Insights for Shaping the Future Analyzing previous monetary experiments offers us significant insights that might influence prospective adjustments in our present monetary system.

The Importance of Flexibility: The rigidity of fixed exchange rate arrangements, like the gold standard, can impede economic progress. Flexibility in adapting to changing economic situations is vital. combining stability and flexibility: Bimetallism illustrates the issue of combining the stability of a fixed exchange rate system with the flexibility needed to absorb economic changes.

The Power of Trust: Alternative money systems rely greatly on trust within communities. Trust in a currency's worth and acceptance by users are vital for the success of any monetary system.

Embracing Technological Innovation: Digital currencies like Bitcoin have proven the potential for creative technology to transform monetary systems. These advancements can provide new opportunities for efficiency and inclusion.

The Need for Adaptability: Historical monetary systems have encountered crises when they couldn't adapt to changing conditions. The capacity to alter monetary policy is vital for stability.

Addressing income disparity: Historical monetary regimes occasionally increased income disparity. Reform attempts should include how monetary policies affect wealth distribution.

Worldwide collaboration: In an interconnected world, worldwide collaboration is crucial for monetary stability. Currency exchange rate systems need safeguards to prevent disruptive volatility.

<u>Environmental Considerations:</u> Modern monetary reforms should also address environmental sustainability, since monetary policy decisions may affect resource use and environmental health.

<u>The Role of Education:</u> Monetary systems are complicated, and public awareness is crucial. Financial education may enable citizens to make educated decisions and hold governments responsible. As we investigate these past monetary systems and their teachings, we develop a clearer grasp of the difficulties and possibilities that lie ahead. In the chapters to follow, we'll expand on these findings to propose potential changes and innovations that might lead to a more egalitarian and stable monetary system. By learning from the past, we may design a better future for our financial world, one that meets the interests of individuals and societies alike.

CHAPTER 5

ALTERNATIVE MONETARY SYSTEM

As we continue our exploration of the future of money, it's vital to evaluate alternative monetary systems that have evolved in recent years. While our existing fiat monetary system has its benefits and shortcomings, other systems offer fresh possibilities for the way we exchange value and conduct financial transactions. In this chapter, we'll introduce you to these alternatives, such as cryptocurrencies, complementary currencies, and asset-backed currencies. We'll assess the advantages and cons of these systems, offering light on their potential to transform the financial environment.

Introduction to Alternative Systems

Unlocking the World of Alternative Currencies In our modern society, money is no longer confined to the tangible domain of paper bills and metal coins. Innovative technology and evolving economic perspectives have given rise to alternative monetary systems.

Let's investigate some of the most noteworthy alternatives:

<u>Cryptocurrencies:</u> The Digital Revolution in Money Cryptocurrencies are possibly the most prominent alternative to traditional fiat currency. They are digital or virtual currencies that use cryptography for security and run on decentralized networks known as blockchains.

Characteristics of Cryptocurrencies:

Cryptocurrencies are decentralized, meaning they are not controlled by a central authority, like a government or central bank. They offer transparency using blockchain technology, letting anybody check transactions. Some well-known cryptocurrencies are Bitcoin, Ethereum, and Ripple.

Advantages of Cryptocurrencies:

Cryptocurrencies offer various advantages, including rapid and low-cost international transactions, security against fraud and counterfeiting, and financial inclusion for the unbanked. They also allow autonomy and control over one's finances.

Obstacles to Cryptocurrencies:

Cryptocurrencies confront obstacles linked to volatility, regulatory uncertainty, and scalability issues. Their value can change dramatically, making them less stable as a store of money. Regulatory concerns differ by jurisdiction, creating uncertainty for users and investment.

Complementary Currencies

Strengthening local economies

Complementary currencies are community-based or local currencies designed to circulate within certain regions or communities. They typically complement the national currency.

Characteristics of Complementary Currencies: Complementary currencies are often issued and administered by local organizations or communities. They encourage spending within the community and try to help local companies. Examples include the Bristol Pound in the UK and BerkShares in Massachusetts.

Advantages of Complementary Currencies: Complementary currencies improve local economic resilience, help small enterprises, and develop community relationships. They can be developed with specific social or environmental goals in mind, such as lowering carbon emissions.

Challenges of Complementary Currencies: These currencies may have little acceptance outside their respective communities. Scaling them to a national or global level might be tough. Managing their stability and controlling inflation can also be hard.

Asset-Backed Currencies
Money with intrinsic value Asset-backed currencies are connected to tangible things

like gold, silver, or other commodities. These assets provide an underpinning that gives the money its inherent worth.

Characteristics of Asset-Backed Currencies:

Unlike fiat currencies, which have value based on government edicts, asset-backed currencies get their value from the assets they represent. Historically, gold and silver were frequent backings for currencies.

Advantages of Asset-Backed Currencies:

Asset-backed currencies can offer stability and prevent governments from issuing excessive amounts of money. They typically establish faith in the currency's value because it is related to something substantial.

Challenges of Asset-Backed Currencies:

Managing the supply of the backing assets can be problematic, especially if the demand for the currency exceeds the available assets. Transitioning from fiat to asset-backed currencies can also be logistically hard.

Pros and Cons of Alternative Systems

Weighing the options Alternative monetary systems offer a range of possibilities and advantages, but they also come with their own set of obstacles. Let's assess the benefits and cons of various systems, considering variables like security, stability, and decentralization.

Pros of Alternative Systems

Decentralization: Cryptocurrencies and certain complementary currencies function on decentralized networks, decreasing the influence of central authority and increasing autonomy.

Transparency: Cryptocurrencies, in particular, offer transparent and immutable transaction records on blockchain technology, boosting security and trust.

Innovation: Alternative systems drive innovation in financial technology, opening doors to new possibilities for payments, smart contracts, and financial inclusion.

Financial Inclusion: Complementary currencies and some cryptocurrencies can enable access to financial services for unbanked communities, fostering financial inclusion.

Diversification: Asset-backed currencies can offer a buffer against fiat currency devaluation, offering diversification in investment portfolios.

Cons of Alternative Systems Volatility: Cryptocurrencies are recognized for their price volatility, which might make them less suitable as a steady store of wealth or medium of exchange.

Regulatory issues: The regulatory landscape for cryptocurrencies is unknown and differs by nation, causing legal and compliance issues.

<u>Lack of Acceptance:</u> Complementary currencies may have low acceptance outside their respective communities, limiting their utility.

<u>Scalability:</u> Cryptocurrencies often experience scalability difficulties, leading to longer transaction processing times and higher fees during peak demand.

<u>Transition Complexity:</u> Transitioning from fiat to asset-backed currencies can be logistically hard, necessitating the management of underlying assets.

<u>Security Concerns:</u> All alternative systems are susceptible to security concerns, such as hacking, fraud, and theft, which can pose dangers to users and investors.

<u>Stability Issues:</u> Maintaining stability, whether it's the stability of bitcoin values or the value of asset-backed currencies, can be tough.

<u>Regulatory Uncertainty:</u> The regulatory landscape for cryptocurrencies is continuously shifting and can affect their legality, adoption, and use.

<u>Potential for Speculation:</u> Cryptocurrencies can attract speculative trading, resulting in price bubbles and market instability.

<u>Environmental Concerns:</u> Some cryptocurrencies have sparked concerns about their energy consumption and environmental impact due to the computing power necessary for mining. As we negotiate the evolving terrain of alternative monetary systems, it's evident that each system has its own unique traits and possible benefits. However, they also come with their own obstacles and uncertainties. In the chapters to follow, we'll investigate how these alternate systems can survive with, complement, or even modify our current monetary system. By recognizing the trade-offs and possibilities, we may work towards a financial world that best meets the interests of individuals and society in the digital age.

CHAPTER 6

THE HUMAN COST OF DAMAGED FINANCES

In our journey to grasp the complexities of the monetary system, it's vital to return our emphasis to its most critical element: humans. The monetary system's health and stability significantly impact individuals and their financial well-being. In this chapter, we'll look into the personal finance issues that many individuals confront within the existing monetary system. We'll also hear the experiences of real people who have been affected by financial crises, shining light on the human cost of damaged finances.

Personal Finance Challenges in the Current System

Navigating the Financial Landscape The current monetary system, with its intricacy and faults, can provide substantial hurdles for individuals striving to guarantee their financial destiny.

Let's analyze some of the biggest personal finance difficulties under this system:

1. Inflation Eroding Purchasing Power:

Inflation, the progressive increase in the costs of goods and services over time, can slowly undermine the purchasing power of people's money. For people on fixed incomes or with limited chances for salary development, rising costs might make it increasingly difficult to buy basic commodities such as housing, healthcare, and education.

2. Income Stagnation: Many individuals have suffered income stagnation or modest salary growth over the years, even as the cost of living has continued to climb. This issue might leave people struggling to make ends meet, save for the future, or invest in their personal development.

3. Debt Burdens: Access to credit is a double-edged sword. While it might provide financial freedom, excessive debt can become a burden. High interest rates on credit cards and loans can trap individuals in a cycle of debt, making it challenging to achieve financial security.

4. Limited Access to Financial Services:

Not everyone has equal access to financial services and goods. Underserved and marginalized populations typically lack access to inexpensive financial services, making it difficult for them to save, invest, or develop credit.

5. Retirement Uncertainty:

Planning for retirement has become increasingly complex in a world where traditional pension systems are less frequent and individuals are responsible for managing their retirement assets. Market volatility and low interest rates can add uncertainty to retirement planning. <u>**6. Healthcare costs:**</u> In many nations, healthcare expenses continue to climb, placing a huge financial burden on individuals and families. Even people with health insurance may face large deductibles and out-of-pocket payments.

<u>Case Studies of Individuals Affected by Financial Crises:</u> Real Stories of Struggle and Resilience To comprehend the human cost of damaged finances, we must listen to the accounts of individuals who have navigated financial crises within the current monetary system. These real-life case studies demonstrate the problems people confront and their desire to overcome them.

Case Study 1: Jane's Battle with Medical Bills:

Jane, a single mother of two, faced a financial dilemma when her younger child was diagnosed with a persistent medical condition. Despite having health insurance, the out-of-pocket payments for specialist treatments and medications were overwhelming. Jane had to dive into her small savings, take on an additional job, and rely on crowdsourcing to finance the rising medical expenditures. Her tale demonstrates the financial hardship that healthcare bills can take on families, even when they have insurance.

Case Study 2: Mark's Student Loan Struggles:

Mark pursued his desire for further education, taking on student debts to pay for his college studies. After graduation, he entered a competitive labor market and struggled to find secure employment. With school loan installments looming and limited income, Mark faced rising debt and the continual worry of making ends meet. His tale underlines the difficulty many young adults encounter when managing student loan debt in an uncertain job environment.

Case Study 3: Maria's Retirement Dilemma: Maria worked diligently all her life, saving for retirement with the aim of enjoying her golden years. However, the financial crisis of 2008 took out a significant amount of her retirement assets. With limited time to recover before retirement, Maria had to reassess her retirement plans,

delay her retirement age, and adapt her living expectations. Her story underscores the vulnerability of retirement funds to market volatility.

Case Study 4: Carlos and Access to Financial Services:

Carlos, a resident of a low-income community, struggled to acquire affordable banking services. Without a bank account, he relied on check-cashing businesses and payday lenders, paying hefty fees for basic financial operations. Carlos's experience underscores the financial difficulties that marginalized groups confront owing to limited access to traditional banks.

Case Study 5: Emily's Credit Card Debt Spiral:

Emily, a recent college graduate,

accumulated credit card debt while covering living expenses and student loan payments. High interest rates and late fines soon compounded her debt, making it difficult to make any headway in paying it off.

Emily's tale emphasizes the problems of managing credit card debt and the impact of high interest rates on financial security. These case studies reflect only a handful of the innumerable individuals who have suffered financial problems within the current monetary system.

Their stories demonstrate the tenacity and determination of those seeking to overcome hardship. It's vital to understand that financial issues can affect anyone, regardless of their background or circumstances. As we evaluate potential changes and innovations in the chapters ahead, we must put these real-life experiences at the center of our conversations. Ultimately, the goal is to build a monetary system that better serves the interests of individuals and communities, lowering the human cost of broken finances.

CHAPTER 7

REFORMING THE MONETARY SYSTEM

Having gone through the complicated web of our current monetary system, its obstacles, and the human experiences of those touched by financial crises, it's time to shift our attention to prospective remedies. Reforming the monetary system is not just a theoretical exercise; it's a pathway to establishing a more egalitarian and stable financial world. In this chapter, we will explore a range of reforms that can address the faults of the current system and discuss the possibility of a monetary system that serves the needs of individuals and societies more effectively.

Propose Reforms for the Current System: Pathways to Improvement

Our current monetary system, while durable in many ways, faces serious difficulties. To develop a more egalitarian and stable monetary system, we must consider a range of measures that can address these difficulties. Let's investigate some potential reforms:

1. Monetary Policy Transparency:

Enhancing trust and accountability One crucial reform is to improve the transparency of monetary policy decision-making. Central banks should explain their goals, strategies, and decision-making processes more transparently to the public. This enhanced transparency can help develop trust and confidence in the monetary system.

Benefits: Greater transparency can reduce uncertainty in financial markets, improve public understanding of monetary policy, and boost accountability.

2. Financial Education: Empowering Individuals Promoting financial education is vital to empowering individuals to make educated financial decisions. Educational programs can help people comprehend basic financial principles, such as budgeting, saving, and investing. Financial literacy can lead to more responsible financial conduct and increased resilience against financial crises.

Benefits: Financially educated people are better equipped to manage their resources, plan for the future, and avoid financial hazards.

3. Reducing Income Inequality:

Addressing wealth disparities Reforms should target income disparity by establishing policies that encourage equitable wealth distribution. This may include progressive taxes, social safety nets, and targeted support for poor populations. The goal is to establish a more fair distribution of economic opportunities and resources.

Benefits: Reducing income disparity can lead to a more stable and harmonious society, with fewer differences in access to education, healthcare, and financial possibilities.

4. Financial Inclusion: Expanding access to services To ensure that all people have access to financial services, changes should focus on fostering financial inclusion. This may involve boosting the availability of inexpensive banking services, expanding access to credit, and supporting initiatives to bring marginalized populations into the financial mainstream.

Benefits: Financial inclusion may empower underprivileged people, reduce poverty, and encourage economic growth.

5. Sustainability Integration:

Environmental Considerations in Policy

Incorporating environmental factors into monetary policy can enhance sustainability. This can involve examining the environmental impact of monetary decisions and supporting investments in green technologies and enterprises.

Benefits: Sustainability-focused monetary policy can contribute to environmental preservation and a more resilient economy in the face of climate change.

6. Digital Currency Innovation:

Exploring new possibilities Innovations in digital currencies, such as central bank digital currencies (CBDCs) and stablecoins, offer prospects for efficiency and financial inclusion. Exploring the creation of secure and widely available digital currencies can be part of reform initiatives.

Benefits: Digital currencies can cut transaction costs, expand financial access, and enable faster and more secure cross-border transactions.

Discuss the potential for a more equitable and stable monetary system. A Vision for the Future As we examine these prospective reforms, we must also anticipate the attributes of a more egalitarian and stable monetary system. What could it look like, and how would it better serve the needs of individuals and societies?

1. Economic Stability: A reformed monetary system should prioritize economic stability, seeking to lessen the frequency and severity of financial crises. This includes steps to prevent excessive speculation, reduce unsustainable debt levels, and promote responsible financial activities.

2. Equitable Wealth Distribution: A more equal monetary system tries to eliminate income and wealth inequities. It involves policies that guarantee all people have the opportunity to use financial services, invest, and participate in economic progress.

3. Financial Inclusion: Financial inclusion is the cornerstone of a reformed system. It means that every individual, regardless of their background, has access to inexpensive and safe financial services. This fosters economic resilience and empowerment.

4. Environmental Sustainability: The monetary system of the future should integrate environmental sustainability into its policies. It should examine the impact of monetary decisions on the environment and stimulate investments in sustainable technologies and practices.

5. Technological advancements:

Incorporating technological improvements is vital. A reformed monetary system should harness advancements in digital currencies, blockchain technology, and financial technology to boost efficiency, cut costs, and enhance security.

6. Transparency and Accountability:

Transparency and accountability are key. A reformed system promotes clear communication of monetary policy choices, free access to financial information, and procedures for holding financial institutions accountable for their activities.

7. Financial Literacy:

Financial literacy is fostered through educational activities that empower individuals to make informed financial decisions. A reformed system understands the role of financial education in fostering economic resilience.

8. Environmental Considerations:

Environmental sustainability is integrated into monetary policy decisions, with an emphasis on lowering the ecological impact of financial activities and fostering responsible environmental actions.

9. Inclusive Growth: The ultimate goal of a reformed monetary system is inclusive economic growth. It guarantees that the advantages of economic development are shared more equally among all members of society. In conclusion, revamping the monetary system is not a faraway dream but a tangible road toward establishing a financial world that better serves the interests of individuals and societies.

By implementing a combination of reforms that address transparency, financial education, income inequality, financial inclusion, sustainability, and technological improvements, we may strive toward a more egalitarian and stable monetary system. This vision for the future envisions a world where financial well-being is within reach for everyone, where financial crises are less frequent and less severe, and where economic growth benefits all members of society. Through united efforts and a dedication to good change, this vision may become a reality.

CHAPTER 8

THE POWER OF FINANCIAL EDUCATION

In our investigation of financial institutions and their impact on individuals and society, one crucial component stands out as a cornerstone to financial well-being: education. Financial education is not simply a luxury; it is a basic tool that helps individuals negotiate the intricacies of the modern financial landscape. In this chapter, we will delve into the importance of financial literacy, understand why it matters for everyone, and explore ideas for enhancing financial education to build a more financially resilient and secure future. Importance of Financial Literacy Unlocking financial empowerment Financial literacy is the foundation upon which individuals can build a secure and prosperous financial future. It comprises the knowledge and abilities needed to make informed financial decisions, manage money effectively, and plan for the future. Let's investigate why financial knowledge is so crucial: 1. Informed Decision-Making Financial literacy gives individuals the knowledge to make educated financial decisions. Whether it's choosing the correct savings account, comprehending the conditions of a mortgage, or assessing investment opportunities, informed choices can greatly impact financial well-being. 2. Budgeting and Money Management Budgeting is a key skill that helps individuals track their income and expenses. Financial literacy provides the tools to design and maintain a budget, ensuring that spending matches financial goals and priorities. 3. Debt Management Managing debt is a vital element of financial literacy. Understanding interest rates, payback terms, and measures for lowering debt can help individuals avoid the traps of excessive debt and high-interest payments. 4. Savings and Investment Financial literacy enables consumers to make informed decisions about saving and investing. It entails understanding the risk and return associated with various investment options, such as stocks, bonds, and real estate. 5. Retirement Planning Planning for retirement is a hard undertaking that demands financial understanding. Individuals must grasp concepts like compound interest, retirement account alternatives, and techniques for accumulating a retirement nest egg. 6. Protection Against Scams and Fraud Financial literacy includes information about frequent financial scams and fraud. It helps individuals spot and reject fraudulent activities that could lead to financial loss. 7. Building financial resilience Financial literacy empowers individuals with the tools to weather financial obstacles and failures. It enables individuals to build emergency reserves, manage unexpected bills, and plan for emergencies. 8. Achieving Financial Goals Ultimately, financial literacy helps individuals work toward their financial goals, whether it's buying a home, starting a business, supporting school, or reaching financial independence. Strategies for Improving Financial Education: Empowering Individuals and Communities Recognizing the importance of financial literacy, efforts to improve financial education must be a shared duty of individuals, educational institutions, policymakers, and financial institutions. Here are ideas for boosting financial education: 1. Inclusion in School Curricula Integrating financial education into school curricula is a vital step. Starting early helps develop a good foundation for financial literacy. Topics can include basic budgeting, saving, investing, and understanding interest. Benefits: Comprehensive financial education in schools guarantees that all children have access to fundamental financial knowledge, regardless of their background. 2. Workplace Financial Education Employers can play a crucial role in encouraging financial literacy among their employees. Offering courses, information, and access to financial consultants as part of employee perks can empower people to make informed financial decisions. Benefits: Workplace financial education can lead to greater employee morale, lower financial stress, and increased productivity. 3. Online Resources and Apps Leveraging technology is an excellent technique to reach a wide audience. Online services, applications, and websites can provide interactive tools and information about budgeting, investing, and managing debt. Benefits: Online resources are accessible to anyone with an internet connection, making financial education widely available. 4. Community Outreach Community organizations and nonprofits can organize financial literacy training and events. These projects can target marginalized populations, providing them with vital financial education materials. Benefits: Community-based financial education initiatives promote inclusion and equity by reaching those who may have limited access to traditional educational resources. 5. Financial Literacy Campaigns Public awareness campaigns can promote the importance of financial literacy and lead individuals to relevant resources. These initiatives can be led by governments, charities, and financial institutions. Benefits: Financial literacy initiatives establish a culture of financial responsibility and inspire individuals to seek out educational opportunities. 6. Mobile Apps and Gamification Mobile apps and gamification tactics can make learning about finance engaging and fun. Interactive games and simulations can help individuals practice financial decision-making in a risk-free setting. Benefits: Gamification appeals to varied learning styles and encourages active engagement in financial education. 7. Collaboration with Financial Institutions Financial firms have a vested interest in fostering financial literacy. Collaboration between banks, credit unions, and educational institutions can result in personalized financial education programs. Benefits: Financial firms may contribute real-world insights and resources, making financial education more practical and relevant. 8. Government Initiatives Governments can play a role by enacting policies that promote financial education. This may involve implementing financial literacy courses in schools, providing funds for educational programs, and incentivizing employers to provide financial education tools. Benefits: Government measures can ensure that financial education is a priority and available to all individuals. 9. Continuous Learning Financial education is a constant process. Encouraging individuals to engage in continual learning and seek out opportunities to increase their financial knowledge is crucial. Benefits: Continuous learning builds financial empowerment and adaptation in an ever-changing financial landscape. 10. Tailored Education for Vulnerable Populations Recognizing that vulnerable populations may confront particular financial issues, designing financial education programs to address their specific needs is vital. This may involve linguistic accessibility, cultural sensitivity, and tailored resources. Benefits: Tailored instruction ensures that financial literacy activities are inclusive and effective for all groups. In conclusion, financial education is a strong instrument that empowers individuals to make informed financial decisions, navigate complex financial systems, and achieve their financial goals. By incorporating financial literacy into schools, workplaces, communities, and internet resources, we can develop a more financially educated and resilient society. Empowering individuals with financial education is not only a matter of personal responsibility; it is a collaborative undertaking that benefits individuals, communities, and society as a whole. As we work toward a more equitable and secure financial environment, financial education serves as a cornerstone of financial empowerment and well-being.

CONCLUSION

As we end our investigation of the complexity of the monetary system, we find ourselves standing at a crossroads junction where history meets the present and the present affects the future. Our trip has brought us through the meandering corridors of economic history, illuminating the strengths and weaknesses of the financial world in which we live. Now, as we say farewell to these pages, let us, once more, focus on the necessity of tackling the difficulties that lurk inside the existing monetary system and the unlimited possibility for positive change.

Reiterating the Importance

The Heartbeat of Our Society The monetary system, frequently functioning in the background, is the lifeblood of our contemporary civilization. It orchestrates the rhythm of our everyday lives, from the groceries we buy to the goals we follow. It determines the prices we pay, the interest rates we bear, and the possibilities we grasp. It's a quiet force that impacts every area of our lives, creating the landscape of our collective dreams. Yet, as we have learned, this seemingly almighty machine is not resistant to defects and problems. The dark specters of inflation, income disparity, financial instability, and opacity stalk the halls of our economic world. These difficulties cannot be pushed under the rug, for they resound far beyond the areas of economics and into the fundamental fabric of our society and the well-being of individuals. The Universal Impact To underscore the significance of tackling these concerns is not a mere exercise in economic rhetoric but a trumpet cry for communal action.

The implications of a failing monetary system are not isolated to textbooks and boardrooms; they creep into the lives of common people. They appear as decreased buying power, restricted economic mobility, and repressed ambitions. They reverberate in the challenges of families attempting to make ends meet, in the frustration of young adults unable to purchase homes, and in the disillusionment of seniors whose investments lose value. In the course of our journey, we've encountered folks who bore witness to the personal cost of broken finances. Their experiences serve as sharp reminders that the obstacles inside the monetary system are not abstract problems to be analyzed academically but real-life impediments that impact people irrespective of their backgrounds or goals. The personal finance concerns people experience mirror the bigger ones ingrained in the monetary system.

www.ingramcontent.com/pod-product-compliance
Lightning Source LLC
Chambersburg PA
CBHW070904260726
48661CB00004B/1590